TIGERS/
LOS TIGRES

by JoAnn Early Macken

Reading consultant: Susan Nations, M.Ed., author/literacy coach/consultant

WEEKLY (WR) READER®
EARLY LEARNING LIBRARY

Please visit our web site at: **www.earlyliteracy.cc**
For a free color catalog describing Weekly Reader® Early Learning Library's list of high-quality books, call 1-877-445-5824 (USA) or 1-800-387-3178 (Canada). Weekly Reader® Early Learning Library's fax: (414) 336-0164.

Library of Congress Cataloging-in-Publication Data

Macken, JoAnn Early, 1953-
    [Tigers. Spanish & English]
    Tigers = Los tigres / by JoAnn Early Macken.
       p. cm. — (Animals I see at the zoo = Animales que veo en el zoológico)
    Includes bibliographical references and index.
    ISBN 0-8368-4386-X (lib. bdg.)
    ISBN 0-8368-4391-6 (softcover)
    1. Tigers—Juvenile literature. I. Title: Tigres. II. Title.
  QL737.C23M1812   2004
  599.756—dc22   2004043096

This edition first published in 2005 by
Weekly Reader® Early Learning Library
330 West Olive Street, Suite 100
Milwaukee, WI 53212 USA

Copyright © 2005 by Weekly Reader® Early Learning Library

Art direction: Tammy West
Production: Jessica Morris
Photo research: Diane Laska-Swanke
Graphic design: Katherine A. Goedheer
Translation: Tatiana Acosta and Guillermo Gutiérrez

Photo credits: Cover © Preston Garrison/Visuals Unlimited; title, pp. 5, 9, 17, 19, 21
© James P. Rowan; p. 7 © William Muñoz; p. 11 © Cheryl A. Ertelt/Visuals Unlimited;
p. 13 © Kjell B. Sandved/Visuals Unlimited; p. 15 © Joe McDonald/Visuals Unlimited

Printed in the United States of America

1 2 3 4 5 6 7 8 9 09 08 07 06 05 04

Note to Educators and Parents

Reading is such an exciting adventure for young children! They are beginning to integrate their oral language skills with written language. To encourage children along the path to early literacy, books must be colorful, engaging, and interesting; they should invite the young reader to explore both the print and the pictures.

Animals I See at the Zoo is a new series designed to help children read about twelve fascinating animals. In each book, young readers will learn interesting facts about the featured animal.

Each book is specially designed to support the young reader in the reading process. The familiar topics are appealing to young children and invite them to read — and re-read — again and again. The full-color photographs and enhanced text further support the student during the reading process.

In addition to serving as wonderful picture books in schools, libraries, homes, and other places where children learn to love reading, these books are specifically intended to be read within an instructional guided reading group. This small group setting allows beginning readers to work with a fluent adult model as they make meaning from the text. After children develop fluency with the text and content, the book can be read independently. Children and adults alike will find these books supportive, engaging, and fun!

Una nota a los educadores y a los padres

¡La lectura es una emocionante aventura para los niños! En esta etapa están comenzando a integrar su manejo del lenguaje oral con el lenguaje escrito. Para fomentar la lectura desde una temprana edad, los libros deben ser vistosos, atractivos e interesantes; deben invitar al joven lector a explorar tanto el texto como las ilustraciones.

Animales que veo en el zoológico es una nueva serie pensada para ayudar a los niños a conocer cuatro animales fascinantes. En cada libro, los jóvenes lectores conocerán datos interesantes sobre ellos.

Cada libro ha sido especialmente diseñado para facilitar el proceso de lectura. La familiaridad con los temas tratados atrae la atención de los niños y los invita a leer — y releer — una y otra vez. Las fotografías a todo color y el tipo de letra facilitan aún más al estudiante el proceso de lectura.

Además de servir como fantásticos libros ilustrados en la escuela, la biblioteca, el hogar y otros lugares donde los niños aprenden a amar la lectura, estos libros han sido concebidos específicamente para ser leídos en grupos de instrucción guiada. Este contexto de grupos pequeños permite que los niños que se inician en la lectura trabajen con un adulto cuya fluidez les sirve de modelo para comprender el texto. Una vez que se han familiarizado con el texto y el contenido, los niños pueden leer los libros por su cuenta. ¡Tanto niños como adultos encontrarán que estos libros son útiles, entretenidos y divertidos!

— Susan Nations, M.Ed., author, literacy coach,
and consultant in literacy development

I like to go to the zoo.
I see tigers at the zoo.

- - - - - - -

Me gusta ir al zoológico.
En el zoológico veo tigres.

All tigers have dark stripes on light fur. No two tigers have the same stripes.

━ ━ ━ ━ ━ ━ ━ ━

Todos los tigres tienen rayas oscuras sobre un pelaje claro. No hay dos tigres con las mismas rayas.

Some tigers live where it is cold. Their **fur** is long and thick. It helps keep them warm.

- - - - - - - -

Algunos tigres viven donde hace frío. Su **pelaje** es largo y grueso y los ayuda a mantenerse calientes.

**fur/
pelaje**

Some tigers live where it is hot. Their fur blends in with tall grass. Their **prey** cannot see them.

- - - - - - - -

Algunos tigres viven donde hace calor. Su pelaje se confunde con la hierba alta. Sus **presas** no pueden verlos.

Tigers can see well, even at night. They hunt alone in the dark.

- - - - - - -

Los tigres pueden ver bien, hasta de noche. Cazan solos en la oscuridad.

When they hunt, they feel
in the dark with long
whiskers. They make
no noise as they walk.

- - - - - - -

Cuando cazan, buscan
en la oscuridad con sus
largos **bigotes**. No hacen
ruido al caminar.

whiskers/
bigotes

Tigers can hear well.
They twitch their ears
to find sounds.

——————————

Los tigres pueden oír
bien. Mueven las orejas
para encontrar los
sonidos.

Tigers spend most of their time alone.

— — — — — — — —

Los tigres pasan la mayor parte del tiempo solos.

I like to see tigers at
the zoo. Do you?

- - - - - - -

Me gusta ver los tigres en
el zoológico. ¿Y a ti?

Glossary/Glosario

fur — hairy coating of animals

pelaje — pelo de los animales

prey — an animal hunted for food

presa — animal que se caza para comerlo

whiskers — long, bristly hair on an animal's face

bigotes — pelos largos y duros en la cara de los animales

For More Information/Más información

Books/Libros

Greenwood, Elinor. *Rain Forest*. New York: DK Publishing
Macken, JoAnn Early. *African Animals*. *Animal Worlds* (series). Milwaukee: Gareth Stevens, 2002.
Shahan, Sherry. *Feeding Time at the Zoo*. New York: Random House, 2000.
van Eerbeek, Ton. *The World of Baby Animals*. New York: Sterling Publishing, 2001.

Web Sites/Páginas Web

NATIONALGEOGRAPHIC.COM
www.nationalgeographic.com/kids/creature_feature/0012/tigers.html
For fun facts, video, audio, a map, and a postcard

Canadian Museum of Nature
www.nature.ca/notebooks/english/tiger.htm
For a tiger illustration and facts

Index/Índice

About the Author/Información sobre la autora

JoAnn Early Macken is the author of two rhyming picture books, Sing-Along Song and Cats on Judy, and four other series of nonfiction books for beginning readers. Her poems have appeared in several children's magazines. A graduate of the M.F.A. in Writing for Children and Young Adults program at Vermont College, she lives in Wisconsin with her husband and their two sons. Visit her Web site at www.joannmacken.com.

JoAnn Early Macken es autora de dos libros infantiles ilustrados en verso, Sing-Along Song y Cats on Judy, y también de cuatro series de libros de corte realista dirigidos a los lectores principiantes. Sus poemas han sido publicados en varias revistas para niños. Graduada del M.F.A. en Redacción para niños y adultos jóvenes del Vermont College, vive en Wisconsin con su esposo y sus dos hijos. Visita su página Web. www.joannmacken.com.